WATER CREATURES

SHARKS

Brenda Ralph Lewis

GARETH**STEVENS**

GS PUBLISHING

A Member of the WRC Media Family of Companies

Please visit our web site at: **www.garethstevens.com**
For a free color catalog describing Gareth Stevens Publishing's
list of high-quality books and multimedia programs,
call 1-800-542-2595 (USA) or 1-800-387-3178 (Canada).
Gareth Stevens Publishing's fax: (414) 332-3567.

Library of Congress Cataloging-in-Publication Data

Lewis, Brenda Ralph.
    Sharks / Brenda Ralph Lewis. — North American ed.
      p. cm. — (Nature's monsters: Water creatures)
    Includes bibliographical references and index.
    ISBN 0-8368-6178-7 (lib. bdg.)
    1. Sharks—Juvenile literature. I. Title. II. Series.
  QL638.9.L52   2006
  597.3—dc22   2005054178

This North American edition first published in 2006 by
Gareth Stevens Publishing
A Member of the WRC Media Family of Companies
330 West Olive Street, Suite 100
Milwaukee, WI 53212 USA

Original edition and illustrations copyright © 2006 by International Masters Publishers AB.
Produced by Amber Books Ltd., Bradley's Close, 74–77 White Lion Street, London N1 9PF, U.K.

Project editor: Michael Spilling
Design: Joe Conneally

Gareth Stevens editorial direction: Valerie J. Weber
Gareth Stevens art direction: Tammy West
Gareth Stevens production: Jessica Morris

Printed in the United States of America

1 2 3 4 5 6 7 8 9 10 09 08 07 06

Contents

Continents of the World

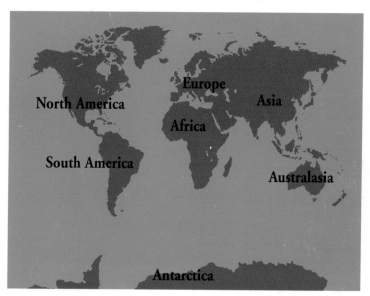

The world is divided into seven continents — North America, South America, Europe, Africa, Asia, Australasia, and Antarctica. In this book, the area where each animal lives is shown in blue, while all land is shown in green.

Words that appear in the glossary are printed in **boldface** type the first time they occur in the text.

Bull Shark

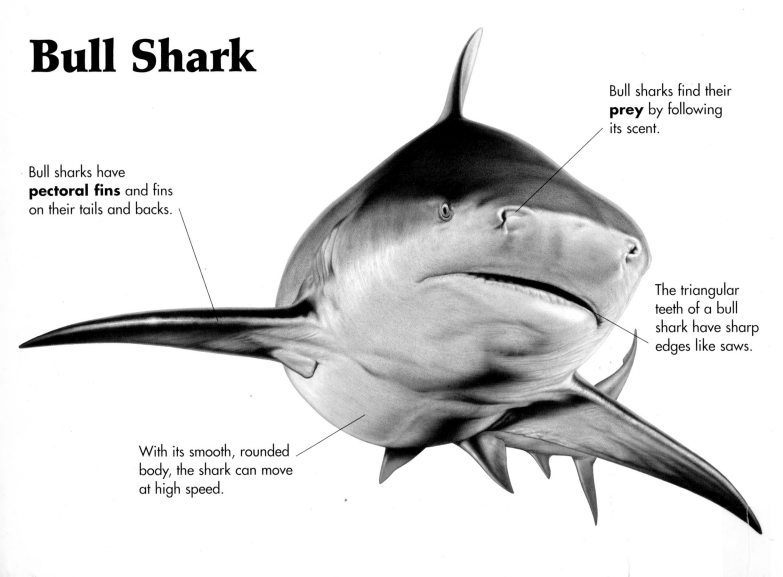

Bull sharks find their **prey** by following its scent.

Bull sharks have **pectoral fins** and fins on their tails and backs.

The triangular teeth of a bull shark have sharp edges like saws.

With its smooth, rounded body, the shark can move at high speed.

Bull sharks are savage killers. The taste of blood excites them. They will eat large fish and mammals such as rays, porpoises, sea lions, and dolphins — as well as other sharks.

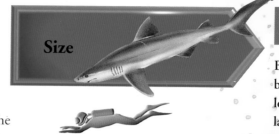

Size

1 A bull shark picks up the **vibrations** of a creature in the water. Following them, the shark soon spots the sea lion.

2 The bull shark puts on a huge burst of speed. With its mouth wide open, it hits the sea lion so hard that the sea lion is killed at once.

3 The water is red with the sea lion's blood. The excited shark bites off big chunks of its body. It does not bother to chew them but swallows each chunk in one piece.

Where in the World

Bull sharks live in the **coastal** waters of Africa, the Americas, Asia, and Australia. They prefer the **tropical** and **subtropical** coasts of these **continents** but do not often enter the **open sea**.

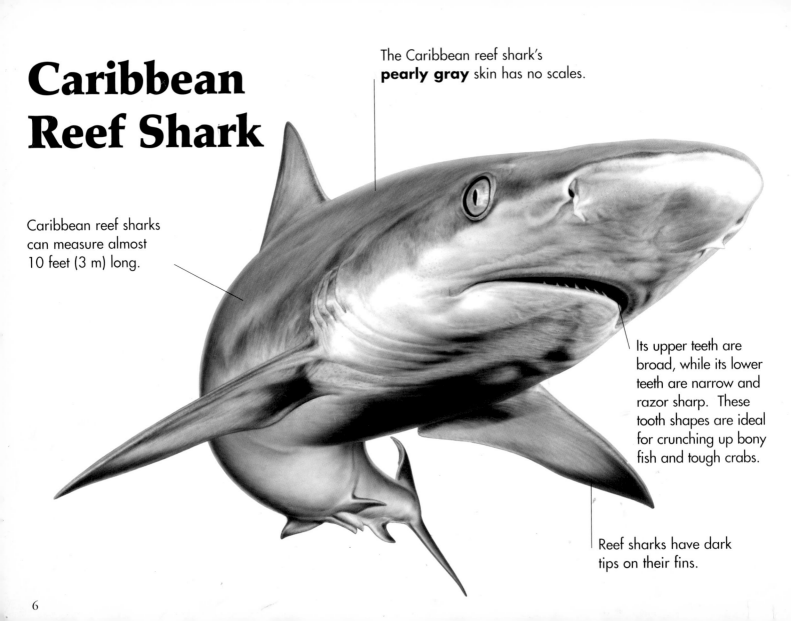

Caribbean Reef Shark

The Caribbean reef shark's **pearly gray** skin has no scales.

Caribbean reef sharks can measure almost 10 feet (3 m) long.

Its upper teeth are broad, while its lower teeth are narrow and razor sharp. These tooth shapes are ideal for crunching up bony fish and tough crabs.

Reef sharks have dark tips on their fins.

Caribbean reef sharks usually prefer to eat small fish and sea turtles. A feeding frenzy can mean they will attack any living thing that gets in their way, however, and that includes humans.

Size

1 Some divers sit on the seabed. They are waiting while a man in a boat above them throws fish scraps into the water. The fish scraps make the water bloody. Caribbean reef sharks come to **investigate**.

2 The sharks start eating the scraps. One diver lifts his arm to point to a fight between two of them. It is a big mistake. A reef shark swoops down and bites the man's forearm.

Where in the World

Caribbean reef sharks live in the coastal waters of the Americas, from Florida and Texas to the north through the Caribbean Sea to Brazil in the south.

Sand Tiger Shark

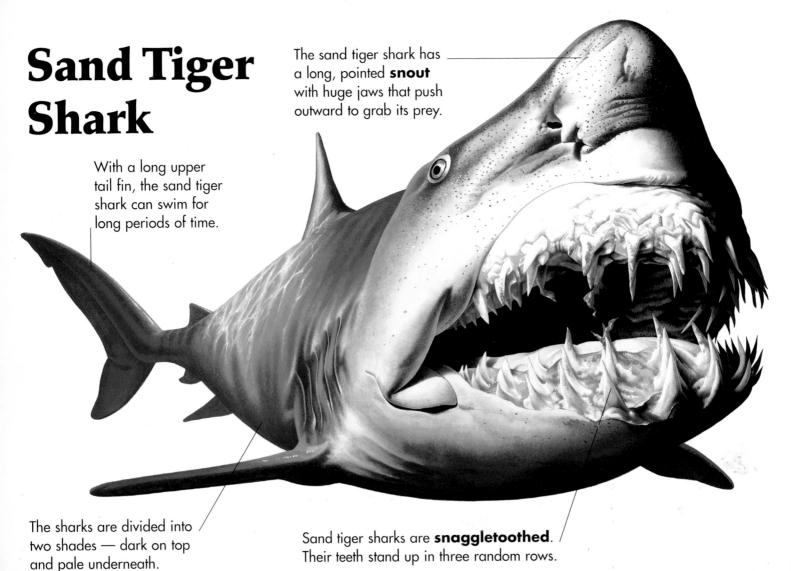

The sand tiger shark has a long, pointed **snout** with huge jaws that push outward to grab its prey.

With a long upper tail fin, the sand tiger shark can swim for long periods of time.

The sharks are divided into two shades — dark on top and pale underneath.

Sand tiger sharks are **snaggletoothed**. Their teeth stand up in three random rows.

Baby sharks can be in great danger while still in their mother's **womb**. They may not even live to be born. Their enemies may be their own brothers or sisters.

Sand tiger sharks can swallow air. The air in its stomach gives the sand tiger shark **buoyancy**. This ability allows it to float in the water without moving.

1 Sand tiger shark mothers produce eggs in egg sacs inside their bodies. When they grow to be 2 inches (6 centimeters) long, the babies break out of their eggs and swim to one of their mother's two wombs.

The babies eat their own **egg sacs** first. This food may not be enough for a big baby. If they are still hungry, they swim into the other womb. Once there, they kill and eat the other 2 baby shark.

Where in the World

Sand tiger sharks live in all of the warmer seas and oceans of the world, except for the eastern Pacific. Most are found in shallow coastal waters.

Great White Shark

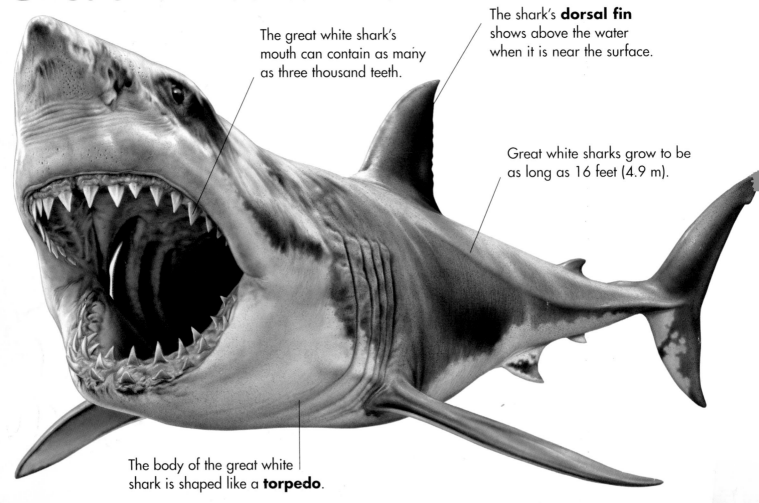

The great white shark's mouth can contain as many as three thousand teeth.

The shark's **dorsal fin** shows above the water when it is near the surface.

Great white sharks grow to be as long as 16 feet (4.9 m).

The body of the great white shark is shaped like a **torpedo**.

The attack of a great white shark on its prey is a terrifying sight. Its huge mouth opens wide to reveal rows of jagged teeth 3 inches (7.5 cm) long.

Size

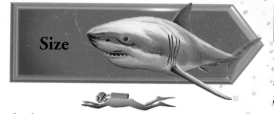

1 The great white shark rushes forward through the water, opening its mouth as it swims. At the same time, it raises its snout out of the way, above the level of its mouth.

2 Just before it hits its prey, the great white pushes its upper jaw forward, making its mouth even bigger.

3 The shark's powerful jaws bite a chunk of flesh out of its prey. To tear off even more, the shark shakes its head from side to side.

Where in the World

Great white sharks live close to the shore in the **temperate** and subtropical areas that lie around North and South America, Africa, Europe, Asia, and Australasia.

11

Tiger Shark

Tiger sharks can grow to between 10 feet (3 m) and 20 feet (6 m) long.

Like the tiger on land, tiger sharks display stripes on their backs.

Unlike other sharks, the tiger shark has a special **gill** behind its eyes that feeds **oxygen** to its eyes and brain.

Tiger sharks have rows of sharp, jagged teeth for tearing their prey apart.

Tiger sharks are fierce **predators** but do not usually attack human beings. Like many sharks, however, they have poor eyesight and can attack other creatures by mistake.

Some strange things have been found in the stomachs of tiger sharks — automobile seats, tires, license plates, tin cans, lumps of coal, and even the head of a crocodile.

1 The surfer cannot see the tiger shark waiting beneath him. His surfboard gets in the way. The shark, looking upward, mistakes the board and the surfer's arms and legs for a turtle. Tiger sharks like eating turtles.

2 The shark waits for the right moment to attack. It **surges** up and bites through the surfboard. The surfer, however, has a lucky escape. The shark does not smell turtle blood. It loses interest and swims away.

Where in the World

The tiger shark lives in the warm waters of the world's seas and oceans. It hunts for food close to land, around coral reefs, and in coastal waters.

Horn Shark

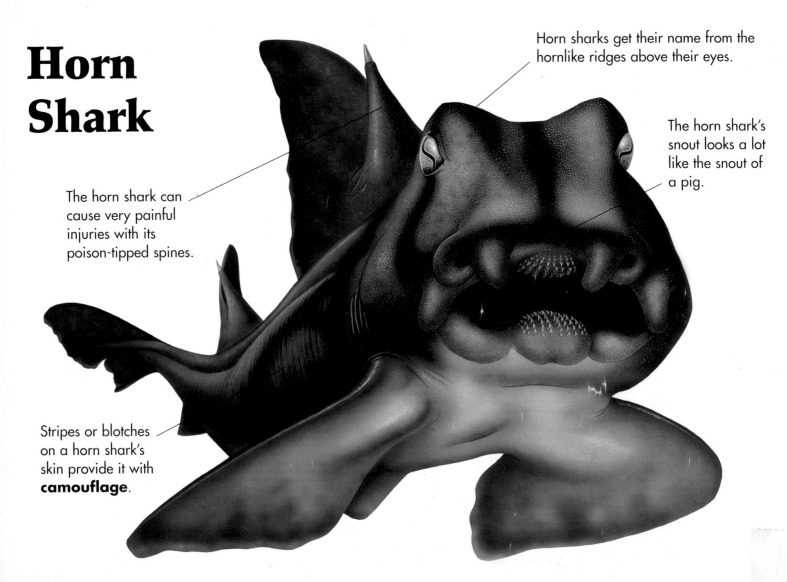

Horn sharks get their name from the hornlike ridges above their eyes.

The horn shark's snout looks a lot like the snout of a pig.

The horn shark can cause very painful injuries with its poison-tipped spines.

Stripes or blotches on a horn shark's skin provide it with **camouflage**.

Horn sharks are one of the smallest of the shark **species**, but they can be dangerous to humans when defending themselves.

1 The diver has fired his **speargun** at the horn shark. With a spear through its body, the shark gushes blood. It will soon die, but not before it strikes back.

Size

2 The dying horn shark lashes out at the diver's leg with its razor-sharp spines, causing a bad gash in the diver's leg. Blood from the diver and the horn shark may attract other sharks.

Where in the World

There are nine species of horn shark. They live up to 650 feet (200 m) beneath the surface of the warm coastal waters of the Indian and Pacific Oceans.

Mako Shark

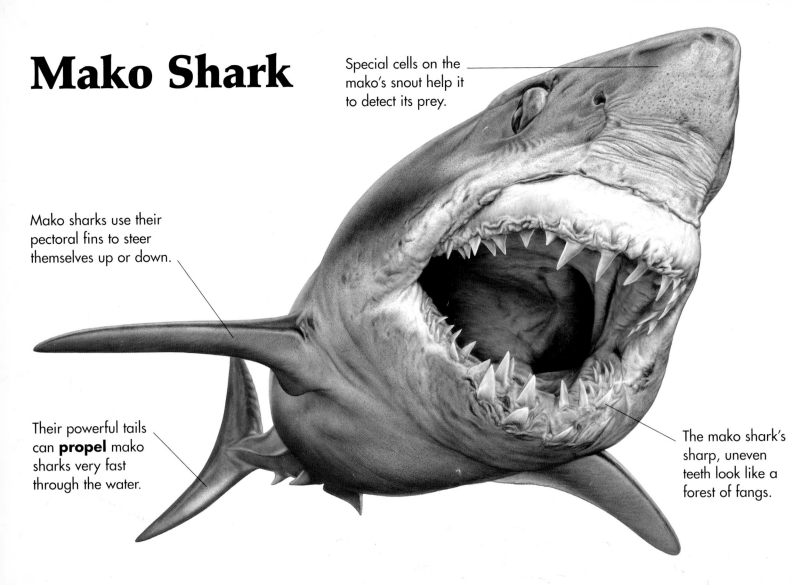

Special cells on the mako's snout help it to detect its prey.

Mako sharks use their pectoral fins to steer themselves up or down.

Their powerful tails can **propel** mako sharks very fast through the water.

The mako shark's sharp, uneven teeth look like a forest of fangs.

The size and tough appearance of mako sharks make them a very popular catch with people who fish for sport. Even when dying, however, they are difficult to tame.

Size

1 This fisherman has caught a mako shark on the hook of his fishing line. The shark fights hard to escape and jumps up out of the water to try to get away. It is still caught, however, so it tries something desperate instead.

2 The mako shark leaps into the boat and seizes the fisherman's leg in its powerful jaws. The fisherman tries to escape. If the shark's jaws close, he could lose his leg.

Where in the World

The mako shark lives mainly in the open sea. Makos prefer the temperate zones. In tropical seas, they swim deep below the surface because the water is cooler there.

17

Cookie Cutter Shark

The cookie cutter's mouth stretches to bite chunks from prey much larger than itself.

The cookie cutter is small. It measures only 20 inches (50 cm) long.

The shark's triangle-shaped teeth slice through flesh like a cookie cutter through dough.

The cookie cutter shark's **luminescent** belly attracts its prey.

Cookie cutter sharks have a glowing belly. The glow lures predators that think the shark will make a tasty meal. The predator then becomes the shark's prey.

Size

Did You Know?

When cookie cutter sharks attack, they use their mouths like suckers to hold onto their victims. They then twist around to take an egg-shaped bite out of the flesh of their prey.

1 The cookie cutter's underbelly glows green. A dolphin becomes interested. It does not think the small shark will cause trouble.

2 Once the dolphin comes close enough, the cookie cutter strikes. Its mouth holds the dolphin's dorsal fin so firmly that it cannot get away. The shark bites a big piece out of the dolphin's fin with its triangular teeth.

3 Its mouth full, the cookie cutter shark moves off to a quiet spot to enjoy its meal. The dolphin is badly injured but still alive.

Where in the World

Cookie cutter sharks are deep-water animals. They live in most of the world's oceans. They prefer warmer, tropical ocean water and can be found in the coastal waters around islands.

Megamouth Shark

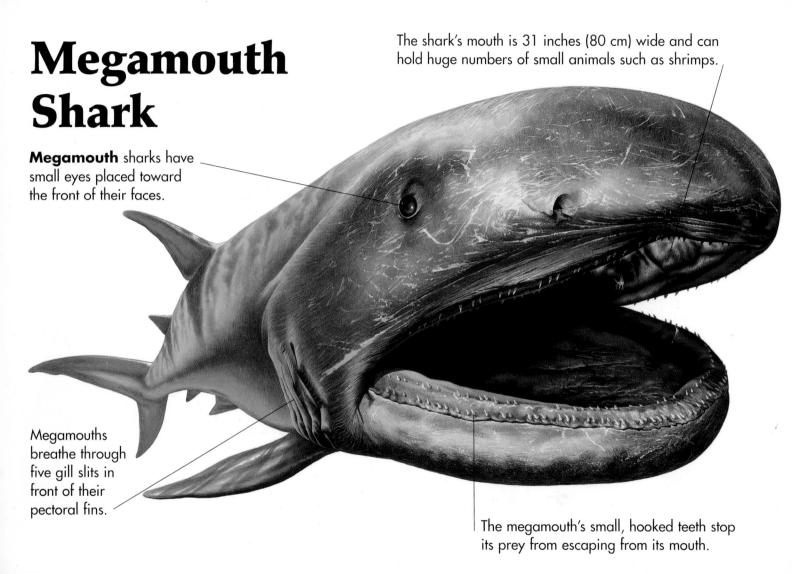

Megamouth sharks have small eyes placed toward the front of their faces.

The shark's mouth is 31 inches (80 cm) wide and can hold huge numbers of small animals such as shrimps.

Megamouths breathe through five gill slits in front of their pectoral fins.

The megamouth's small, hooked teeth stop its prey from escaping from its mouth.

Unlike most sharks, the megamouth shark does not get its food by attacking its prey and tearing it into pieces. It has its own, much less violent way of feeding itself.

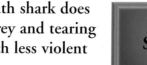

Size

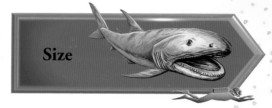

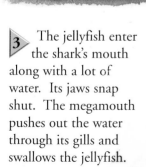

1 The megamouth shark swims along slowly in the ocean deep. **Shoals** of tiny creatures swim nearby. The shark is following them.

2 The megamouth sees some small jellyfish and moves forward with its mouth wide open. The inside of the shark's mouth glows. The jellyfish are attracted by the glow.

3 The jellyfish enter the shark's mouth along with a lot of water. Its jaws snap shut. The megamouth pushes out the water through its gills and swallows the jellyfish.

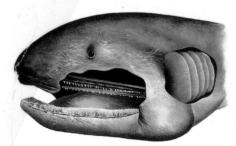

Where in the World

There are only small numbers of megamouth sharks in the world. They live mainly in the warmer waters of the Pacific, Indian, and Atlantic Oceans.

Wobbegong

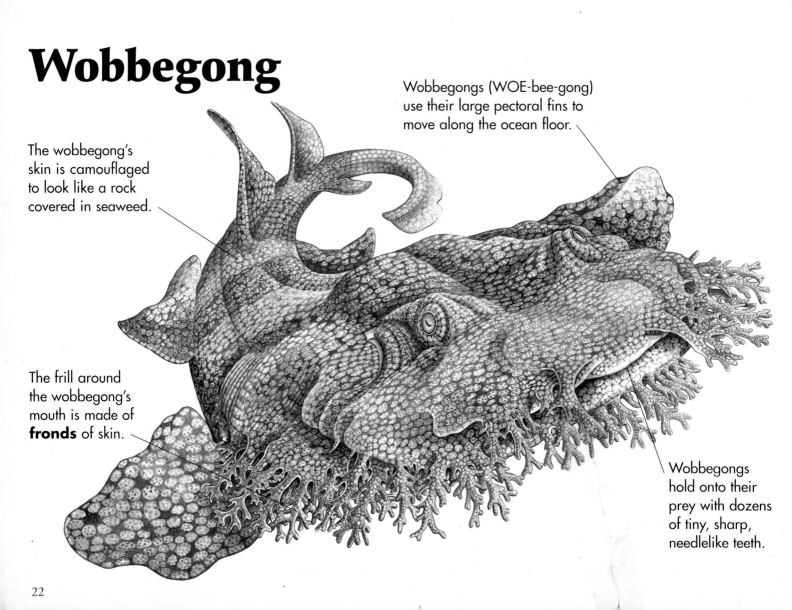

Wobbegongs (WOE-bee-gong) use their large pectoral fins to move along the ocean floor.

The wobbegong's skin is camouflaged to look like a rock covered in seaweed.

The frill around the wobbegong's mouth is made of **fronds** of skin.

Wobbegongs hold onto their prey with dozens of tiny, sharp, needlelike teeth.

22

The wobbegong shark seems lazy and slow. Some divers may think it is not dangerous, but the wobbegong can lash out when disturbed.

Size

1 The wobbegong shark lies on the ocean floor, waiting for its prey to pass by. The diver swims up and tries to examine the shark by pulling its tail.

2 The diver is shocked to find his leg trapped inside the wobbegong's mouth. It has happened so fast that the diver is taken by surprise. The wobbegong sinks its teeth firmly into the diver's leg.

Where in the World

The wobbegong shark lives in the warm waters of the eastern Pacific. It can be found off the coasts of Australia, New Guinea, Indonesia, the Philippines, China, and Japan.

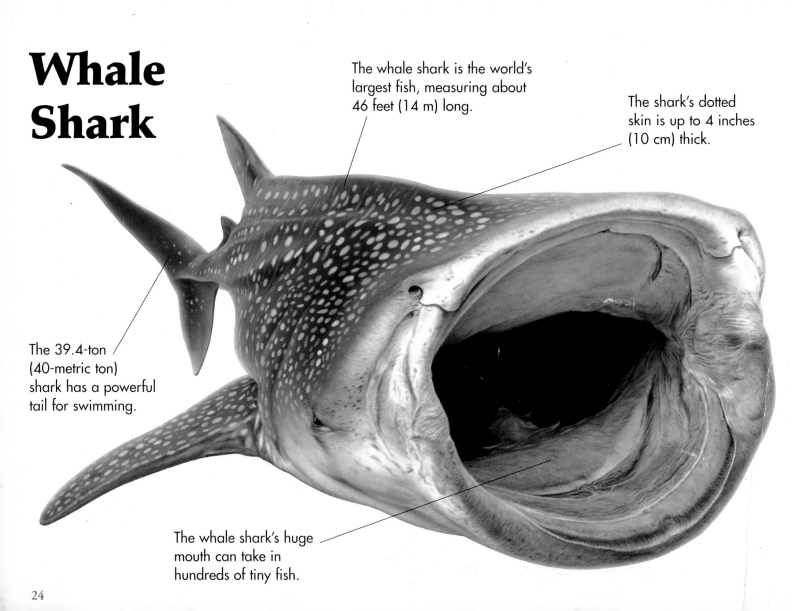

Whale Shark

The whale shark is the world's largest fish, measuring about 46 feet (14 m) long.

The shark's dotted skin is up to 4 inches (10 cm) thick.

The 39.4-ton (40-metric ton) shark has a powerful tail for swimming.

The whale shark's huge mouth can take in hundreds of tiny fish.

In spite of their huge size and enormous mouths, whale sharks are not at all dangerous to swimmers or divers. They pay little attention to human beings nearby.

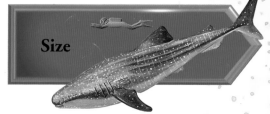

1 The peaceful whale shark does not mind when one of these divers grabs hold of the big dorsal fin on its back. Instead, the whale takes the diver for a ride through the water.

2 The diver could find himself in great danger if the whale shark decides to dive quickly into the depths of the ocean, however. If it decides to move up quickly to the surface again, the diver may also die from the sudden change in water **pressure**.

Where in the World

Whale sharks live in warm waters in the open seas or close to the coasts. They spend most of their time near the surface, where they will find food.

Hammerhead Shark

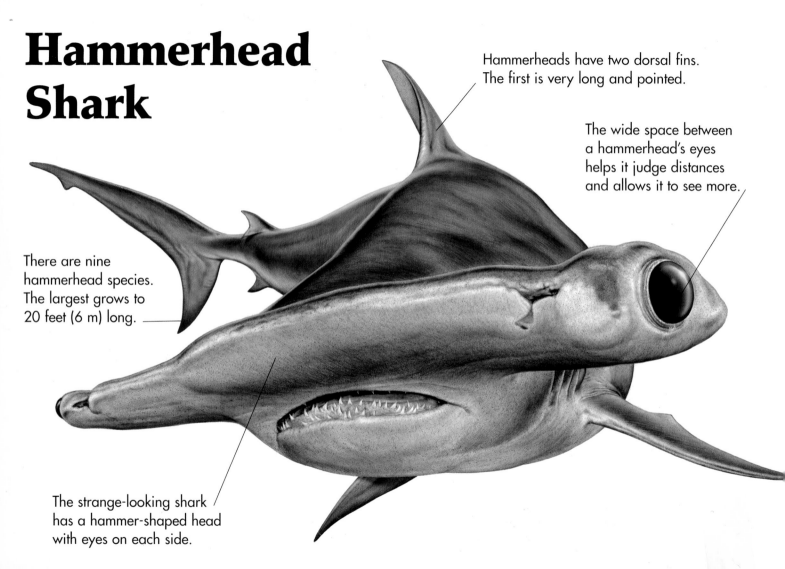

Hammerheads have two dorsal fins. The first is very long and pointed.

The wide space between a hammerhead's eyes helps it judge distances and allows it to see more.

There are nine hammerhead species. The largest grows to 20 feet (6 m) long.

The strange-looking shark has a hammer-shaped head with eyes on each side.

The hammerhead shark's favorite food is the **stingray**. The shark's hammer-shaped head proves very useful in stopping a stingray from getting away before it can be eaten.

Size

1 A stingray lies covered in sand on the ocean bed. It thinks it is hidden from sight. The shark has found it by using its wide-spaced eyes to scan the ocean bed, however. This special vision makes it easy for the shark to find its prey.

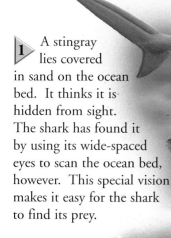

2 The shark moves quickly and holds the stingray down with its wide hammer head. The stingray may struggle, but it cannot stop the shark from biting off pieces of its pectoral fins.

Where in the World

Hammerhead sharks can be found in any of the world's tropical and subtropical oceans. They like the warm, sunlit waters lying above **shelves** on the edge of continents.

Angel Shark

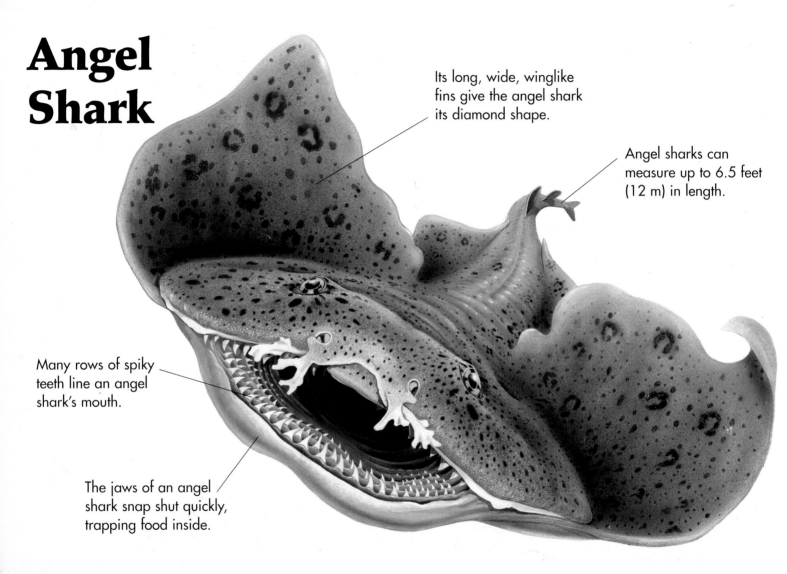

Its long, wide, winglike fins give the angel shark its diamond shape.

Angel sharks can measure up to 6.5 feet (12 m) in length.

Many rows of spiky teeth line an angel shark's mouth.

The jaws of an angel shark snap shut quickly, trapping food inside.

It can be very dangerous to swim too close to an angel shark. It can be even more dangerous to touch it because its very sharp teeth can deliver a nasty bite.

Size

1 Hungry angel sharks bury themselves in the sand and mud of the ocean bed while they wait for prey to pass by. They cannot be seen, except for their eyes and the tops of their backs.

2 This diver wants to see more of the shark. He pokes at it, making the shark angry. It jumps up and sinks its sharp, spiky teeth into the diver's hand.

Did You Know?

Angel sharks are also called fiddlefish because they look like a violin when seen from above. Another name for them is monkfish because they also look like the hoods on a monk's cloak.

Where in the World

There are about twelve different species of angel shark. They live in the coastal waters of the Atlantic and Pacific as well as off the coast of eastern Africa.

Glossary

Aboriginal — describing the first people to live in Australia, the Aborigines

bouyancy — the ability to stay afloat in water

camouflage — the pattern on an animal's skin that helps to hide it

coastal — along a coast where the land meets the sea

continents — the great landmasses on Earth—Africa, North America, South America, Antarctica, Asia, Australasia, and Europe

dorsal fin — the main fin on the back of a fish or shark

egg sacs — bags in which eggs are kept instead of shells

estuaries — areas of rivers where they meet the sea and mix with the salt water

fronds — leaflike strips

gill — the part of an animal used for breathing under water; all fish have gills

investigate — to look at and study

luminescent — shining with light

megamouth — extra large mouth

open sea — water that is far from land

oxygen — gas that makes up one-fifth of the air and is also present in water; animals need oxygen to live

pearly gray — shiny gray like a pearl

pectoral fins — a pair of fins behind the head of a fish or shark that controls the direction it swims

predators — animals that hunt other animals for food

pressure — the weight of the water in a sea or ocean, especially in the deepest parts

prey — an animal hunted for food

propel — cause to move

shelves — places where the seabed suddenly drops away to another level, like a step

shoals — large masses or groups of fish

snaggletoothed — teeth in an uneven line

snout — short, flat nose

speargun — a gun used under water that shoots a spear

species — a group of living things of the same family or type

stingray — a large, flat fish with wide, winglike fins with a sting in its tail; stingrays are related to sharks

subtropical — referring to warm regions of the world with some tropical weather but less rain than tropical areas

surges — rushes

temperate — referring to a climate marked by temperatures that are neither very hot nor very cold

torpedo — a cigar-shaped missile fired by ships and submarines through the sea during wartime

tropical — referring to the warmest regions of the world, with lush plant life and lots of rain

vibrations — back and forward or shaking motions

womb — the place in many animal's bodies where babies grow

For More Information

Books

All About Sharks. All About (series). Jim Arnosky (Scholastic Press)

Best Book of Sharks. Best Book of (series). Claire Llewellyn (Kingfisher)

Shark. DK Eyewitness (series). Miranda MacQuitty (Dorling Kindersley)

Sharkabet: A Sea of Sharks from A to Z. Ray Troll (Westwinds Press)

Sharks: 3-D Book. Discovery Kids (series). (Dutton Juvenile)

What Do Sharks Eat For Dinner? Questions and Answers About Sharks. Scholastic Question & Answer (series). Melvin Berger and Gilda Berger. (Scholastic Reference)

Web Sites

Monterey Bay Aquarium: Children's Page
www.mbayaq.org/efc/efc_smm/smm_resources.asp

National Geographic Kids
www.nationalgeographic.com/kids/creature_feature/0206/sharks.html

Ocean of Know
www.oceanofk.org/sharks/sharks.html

Shocking Sharks
projects.edtech.sandi.net/sessions/sharks

Shark Friends
www.sharkfriends.com

Zoom Sharks: Enchanted Learning Software
www.enchantedlearning.com/subjects/sharks

Index